And Dream She Would

MJ Clements

SQUARE TREE PUBLISHING

www.SquareTreePublishing.com

Copyright © 2023 by MJ Clements

All rights reserved, including the right to reproduction in whole or in part in any form.

For more information about bulk purchases, please contact Square Tree Publishing at info@squaretreepublishing.com.

Illustration by Kailyn Sissom

ISBN 978-1-957293-24-0

Dedication

To my beautiful grandchildren, Eli, Callum, Mylah, and Devlin—you are the inspiration for my writing and the very reason I wrote this book. I pray you will have many of my books to read now and to read to your children and to their children. My love for you will be forever.

In memory of my mom and dad. My mom—my cheerleader in every endeavor I took; my prayer warrior in all of the risks I took and my comforter in all of the disappointments that came my way. Words cannot express how grateful I am—and will always be—for you! My dad—my hero for finding Jesus for our whole household (Acts 16:31). A dreamer at heart who bestowed this upon me. I will follow the dream God has for me! I will always be thankful for you!

I love and miss you both always.

Acknowledgements

To my children, Angela and Evan. Words cannot express the love I have for you both; it is full beyond measure. To my husband—I am blessed to be with you on every adventure we've taken and to experience this life we lead. We're in it together! The things God has done with us, for us, and through us have shown many miracles—the many stories we could tell! Maybe a book to come? Our Memoir. God knew what He was doing when He gave you all to me. I am blessed.

About the Book And Dream She Would

To a little group of women in the northern part of Maine, where my creativity for writing was conceived. The encouragement of a friend (CS), who asked me to create a fun little activity for the women to participate in. Three in the morning, God breathed into my dreams this story in part and so it quietly grew.
Fast forward to twenty something years later, He birthed this story. This is my encouragement for God's children, both young and old, though young at heart. Let God move through your dreams. They can't be forced; they can be unexpected. You can stand in the hope that your dreams can come true, just rest assured to seek Him first. Wait patiently on Him. He has created the dream just right for you. He's faithful…always.

And to my ladies in my Writers' Cohort group at Square Tree Publishing, Melodie, Marlena, Irene, and Lynn—our new beginning as authors has just begun! Your friendship and support are invaluable. I am so thankful for each one of you and look forward to reading all of the books that come forth from here!

Amazee loved to dream.
"If only my dreams could come true!" she said with a sigh.

"Follow your dreams," she'd heard someone say. "But how?" Amazee thought for a moment. "Mom and Dad always say 'Sweet Dreams' to me before I go to sleep. I should start there!"

That night, Amazee jumped into bed and waited for the official words...
"GOOD NIGHT, SWEET DREAMS, AMAZEE!" Mom and Dad gave her a hug and the lights went out.

Just then, Amazee sat right up, pointed her finger to the sky, and proclaimed, "I want to be a movie star!" And with that, she laid her head on her pillow, closed her eyes,

AND
DREAM
SHE
WOULD!

Amazee was up early and ready for the day.
She grabbed a pair of sparkly sunglasses and gave herself a wink as she passed by the mirror.
"Can't keep my fans waiting!" she exclaimed as she slipped them on.

Strutting across the kitchen floor with an unusual sway of the hips, she tossed her fluffy pink boa over her shoulder, her nose up in the air.
"Good grief," her brother said, rolling his eyes.

"Humph!" she said. And out the door she went.

Later that day, Amazee dragged herself to the dinner table and sighed. "I don't feel like a movie star. It's far too feathery and flashy for me!" She flopped into her chair to plan her next attempt at dreaming.

That night, Amazee jumped into bed and waited for the official words...

"GOOD NIGHT, SWEET DREAMS, AMAZEE!" Mom and Dad gave her a hug and the lights went out.

Just then, Amazee sat right up, pointed her finger to the sky, and proclaimed, "I want to be a magician!" And with that, she laid her head on her pillow, closed her eyes,

AND DREAM SHE WOULD!

Amazee was up early, ready for the day. This time, she found her great-grandfather's top hat. It was old and tattered, but she loved how with just one flick she could make it go from flat to full.

POP!

"TAH DAH!" she said proudly.

"LADIES AND GENTLEMEN, MAY I INTRODUCE TO YOU AMAZEE, THE AMAZING MAGICIAN!" she announced as she entered the kitchen.

Her mother clapped and cheered.

"Those aren't even the magic words," her brother corrected.

Amazee squinted at her brother as she walked by. "I'm about to AMAZE everyone! After all, my name IS Amazee!"

And out the door she went.

That evening, she sat in her room holding the tattered top hat and thought, "I didn't feel like a magician." She gently pressed the hat down and set it on the shelf. "I don't like playing tricks!"

So, Amazee jumped into bed and waited for the official words...
"GOOD NIGHT, SWEET DREAMS, AMAZEE!" Mom and Dad gave her a hug and the lights went out.

Just then, Amazee sat right up, pointed her finger to the sky, and proclaimed, "I want to be a ballerina!" And with that, she laid her head on her pillow, closed her eyes,

AND DREAM SHE WOULD!

The next morning, Amazee twirled down the hall to the breakfast table.

"What are you now?" her brother groaned.

"I am a world-renowned ballerina!" She tiptoed across the floor.

"Mom, what is 'world-renowned'?"

"It means to be famous," her mother explained.

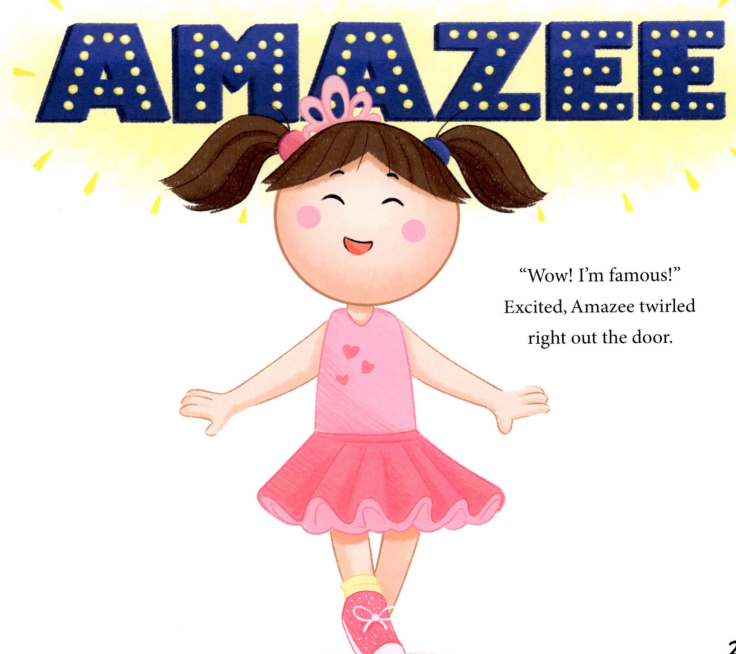

"Wow! I'm famous!" Excited, Amazee twirled right out the door.

That evening as she crawled into bed, she could barely keep her eyes open. "I don't feel like a ballerina. Too much twirling for me." Amazee yawned and closed her eyes.

"Good night, sweet dreams, Amazee," whispered Mom and Dad as they blew her a kiss and the lights went out.

The next morning, Amazee woke up when she heard her mother call, "Amazee! Amazee!" She sat right up.

"OH NO! I DIDN'T PLAN MY DREAM!"

She took long, slow steps to the kitchen.

"Amazee? What's wrong?" her mother asked.

"I didn't plan my dream last night. Now I can't follow my dreams!"

"Aww, AMAZEE!" Her mother gave her a big hug. "It's wonderful you are trying to follow your dreams. But remember to be yourself.

You be YOU!"

Her mother gave her another squeeze. "There is no other Amazee like you!" she said. "And don't ever forget, God created you. He has a plan for you. Your dreams are a part of it. Now, tell me about your dreams, Amazee," her mother said.

"Well, I had a dream about pencils. So, I stuck an extra one in my backpack just in case."

Turned out someone needed one!" Amazee explained.

"Wonderful!" her mother said with a smile.

"A few days later, I became friends with a new student. And I remembered that dream." Amazee smiled.

Although she had no dream planned, she realized she was happy with her dreams just the same.

That night as her mom and dad tucked her in, Amazee said, "I may not want to be a movie star or a magician or even a ballerina, but I am happy to be me—Amazee!"

She hugged her mom and dad extra tight that night.
"Good night, sweet dreams, Amazee!" And the lights went out.

Genesis 40:8b

AND DREAM SHE WOULD!

About the Author

If you've read the playful children's book, **And Dream She Would,** you have met author MJ Clements in some small way. As her character Amazee enthusiastically follows her dreams, it reflects the adventuresome spirit of MJ. "When my two children were young, I traveled to Wisconsin, spending time at Clown Camp on the LaCrosse Campus of Viterbo University. It was one of my greatest privileges to be under the leadership of London's well known mime artist, Nola Rae." As an avid gymnast, MJ has also been an instructor for most of her adult life. Gymnastics gave her independence, and she began developing her own programs. "I loved working with little ones...their imagination is incredible. I especially love seeing their accomplishments."

A travel enthusiast, MJ has had the "travel bug" since her first trip to Texas with her mom. She and her husband, Todd, trekked all over New England and parts of the south. She caught her first glimpse of buffalo and desert life on a trip to the Badlands, got "up close and personal" with a reef shark, explored the Bahamas, Mexico, and the island of Cozumel. "We snorkeled just about every day and saw ruins—and so many iguanas! I loved venturing into the 'cenotes' (underwater caves)—we even ate at a restaurant inside one of the caves." Her adventures don't end there. She has also swung from a trapeze, parasailed, zip lined over the jungle canopy 6,000 feet above sea level, and seen (or heard) countless exotic wildlife. She continues to pursue her passions by writing stories for children of incredible adventures.

When MJ is not exploring the world around her, her world revolves around family. "My grandchildren are the light of my life; they are an integral part of my inspiration to write. I look forward to seeing them grow; to listen to their hearts as their imagination ignites and to hear their own dreams. I'm excited to see what their imprint in this world will be and to watch *their* adventures unfold."

Made in the USA
Columbia, SC
14 October 2024